MW01681408

Embracing Tyler's World

Finding Meaning in a Life That
Doesn't Need Fixing

Paul Harrison
Paperback Edition - First Edition
Published by Floating Balloon Press

© 2026 Paul Harrison. All rights reserved. No part of this publication may be reproduced, stored, or transmitted in any form without prior written permission, except for brief quotations used in reviews or scholarly articles.

Table of Contents

Welcome

Most people move through life as if on an elevator—gliding to milestones without effort or awareness.

With Tyler, it has always been a staircase. Each step built, one at a time—some take longer, some are harder to climb, some remain unbuilt.

What others race past we stop to see, to feel, to celebrate.

Introduction

This isn't a story with neat endings, but one of commitment—hearing what's never spoken, loving what can't be changed.

This book wasn't written to fix anything—or anyone. It exists so you feel less alone. If you care for someone—whether as family, a friend, or a professional—then this story is yours too.

Tyler—autistic, non-speaking, gentle yet fiercely expressive—has taught me that life's deepest connections are found in gestures and routines.

What follows is one parent's reality: improvising, advocating, and cherishing the quiet moments.

I write this as a father—someone who has spent thirty-seven years building a bridge to a son who could not meet me halfway.

Though I share from my perspective, many others have shaped Tyler's happiness—his mother, his siblings, my wife, and the caregivers who have supported him over the years. Their care remains part of his story, even if not detailed here.

There is plenty of humor, but it isn't meant to suggest that parenting a child with profound needs is easy. It's simply how I've survived the hard days and honored the absurd ones.

The first chapters may feel quiet—more reflection than resolution. That's intentional. They lay the groundwork for what's to come.

If you stay with me, the story deepens, the laughter sharpens, and the meaning grows—often in ways readers don't expect.

Tyler, As He Is

Tyler doesn't speak. But he has a way of making himself heard.

Every morning, he waits for me and hands me the remote control—like clockwork. That's his signal: *time to turn on the music.*

And I do.

He's thirty-seven now—a gentle soul with kind eyes and my unfortunate lack of hair. At five foot nine and about one hundred sixty-five pounds, he smiles like he knows something you don't.

People are drawn to him, even if they don't understand why.

Tyler functions at the developmental level of a young child—between ages two and four. He needs help with most daily tasks—dressing, bathing, preparing meals—but he's not helpless. He can buckle his own seatbelt—more on that later—and he navigates familiar places with the instinct of a seasoned traveler. His sense of danger is limited, so childproofing isn't a phase—it's a way of life.

He is non-speaking, but not voiceless. His gestures and expressions speak volumes, reminding me daily that communication isn't limited to words. He remembers things—trivial things, emotional things—that most people miss.

Tyler's world is shaped by repetition, anticipation, and sparks of joy that erupt without warning. It's not always easy to explain. But it's real.

His life has shaped every part of mine—from unexpected joys to the heartbreak of dreams that may never come true.

What follows is a story of tough decisions, moments of surrender, and the times I questioned everything—my choices, my strength, my worth as a parent.

This book is about finding meaning in a life that didn't go according to plan—and discovering that the most important lessons often come from the most unlikely teachers.

One lesson stands out: how to laugh when others might only see struggle—because sometimes the absurd is sacred, and the messiest days hold the most meaning.

Today, I asked Tyler to put on his seatbelt. No movement from the back seat.

I asked again. Nothing but a slight giggle.

Then I turned around. It was already on.

Tyler thought that was funny. So did I.

When the Silence Spoke

Tyler was fourteen months old the morning I knew something was seriously wrong.

Sunlight lit his face as he sat in his car seat on the kitchen floor. His eyes were vacant—as if he wasn't there with me anymore.

That morning has stayed with me. But Tyler's story began much earlier.

Tyler entered our lives as our second child—with all the excitement and dreams that come with a new baby, and none of the preparation for what was coming.

His first two years moved slowly. Many milestones—steps, words, laughter—were missed or came late. Time moved differently, as if Tyler were attuned to a frequency the rest of us couldn't hear.

As parents, we couldn't ignore the quiet concern that crept into our thoughts. Were we overreacting, or was something wrong?

During this period, Tyler's interactions with the world followed their own logic. His fascination with patterns and repetition wasn't just quirky—it was constant, consuming.

We didn't understand. We needed answers.

That vacant stare sent us searching—first to pediatricians, then to specialists.

The word "autism" was introduced—a term we were only beginning to understand. The diagnosis came years later, bringing both revelation and relief.

Those first two years became the foundation—built not in leaps and bounds but in the uneasy rhythm of progress and setbacks.

That gaze became our compass—pointing us toward questions we weren't prepared to ask, and paths we never imagined we'd walk.

That moment sent us searching—first close to home, then to Boston.

Naming What We Couldn't Fix

We turned to Boston in search of answers.

Neurologists watched Tyler during appointments—his movements, his responses, how he did or didn't engage with the world. They searched for patterns, signs of growth—anything that might explain what we were seeing.

"He's on his own timeline," they told us. "Progress, no matter the pace, is encouraging." And Tyler was making progress—slow, unpredictable, but real.

At age three, when most children are forming sentences, he stood in our backyard, pointed skyward, and said, "Plane in sky." His voice, though rarely heard, was filled with wonder.

Hearing his voice sparked a small, unexpected hope—that more words might follow.

This fleeting phrase became a milestone—a bridge between his inner world and ours. Three words that showed us he was in there, watching, connecting.

Hidden in this small victory was an absence—he never said Mom or Dad. But he has always expressed love in his own way, like placing his hand in mine. That speaks volumes.

The few words he had said faded before his fourth birthday. As parents, we held onto that memory—"Plane in sky"—hoping for his limited speech to return. It never did.

The specialists who once expressed hope now struggled to explain the setbacks. The changes in his speech and behavior were obvious—the reasons for the changes less so.

The silence that replaced his words drove us to search for reassurance that we hadn't lost him.

We attended a conference where an expert explained the regression that often occurs between ages three and four in children with autism. It was a piece of information we hoped might help explain Tyler's loss of speech.

Around this time, Tyler's diagnosis was confirmed—autism. With a name, we believed, would come access to therapies, interventions, and tools to help him build essential life skills. It felt like the first step toward helping him grow.

We soon realized believing was not enough.

Parenting Without a Map

The diagnosis of autism brought mixed emotions—relief in finally having a name for what we were seeing and fear about what it meant for Tyler's future.

The professionals offered insights. Autism, they explained, was a spectrum—every child different, every path unique.

What we heard beneath the careful phrasing was: "We have no idea what to tell you about Tyler's future."

The label provided a starting point, but did little to predict what lay ahead.

By age four, Tyler moved with the relentless activity of an Energizer Bunny—unstoppable, unpredictable, utterly himself.

Left unattended, he would roam the house, putting himself in harm's way. He'd climb stairs, open cabinets, pull objects from shelves—oblivious to the danger they posed. Electrical outlets, sharp corners, cleaning supplies—everything was a potential hazard.

We followed his movements, scanning rooms with the vigilance of air traffic controllers—always trying to stay one step ahead of a possible crisis. Our house felt less like a home and more like a tactical zone. We didn't decorate anymore—we barricaded.

Our vigilance became second nature. The emotional toll was significant. Every move carried the weight of what might happen if we looked away. Each of us navigated this path, bound by a common thread: fear of what lay ahead.

The fear wasn't only for Tyler, but also for us—parents learning on the fly.

As we struggled to meet Tyler's needs at home, the question of where he would learn beyond our walls loomed larger. And what lay ahead wasn't just uncertainty—it was resistance—from the very systems meant to support him.

The Door That Stayed Closed

As we began to make peace with the diagnosis, a new challenge emerged—one we didn't see coming.

As Tyler neared age five, we started looking for the right school. During that process we learned our town had never served an autistic student with his level of disability.

The local school expressed confidence they could create a program for him, but something felt off. They were pushing us to keep him local—yet couldn't tell us what that program would look like.

When we asked for details, we received only vague promises.

Skeptical the school system could meet Tyler's needs, we began searching for alternatives.

Beyond our town's limits, we found a school that seemed to offer more than hollow assurances—a place designed for children like Tyler.

With cautious hope, we arranged to visit.

Our first impression of the school was positive. Walking down the halls, we saw compassionate staff engaging with students in ways that felt right. A brief demonstration of their learning techniques was compelling.

The meeting went well, and our hope grew—maybe we had found a place where Tyler could learn and thrive.

Just as optimism began to bloom, they delivered the blow: "Tyler does not fit our profile. We are not equipped to meet his needs."

We walked in believing we held the reins. But as the conversation unfolded, it became painfully clear we were never the ones making the final decision.

Our follow-up questions revealed the truth. Tyler's autism was more severe than any student they had ever served.

Hearing their rejection was devastating—if even specialized schools couldn't help him, what would?

The hope we'd walked in with collapsed into disappointment and loss. We walked slowly to our car, stunned, unsure what came next.

As we sat there trying to absorb the blow, another dilemma surfaced: a business trip I'd scheduled weeks earlier for that afternoon. Not thinking clearly, I drove directly to the airport.

I should have canceled the trip. I should have stayed with my family as we processed the heartbreak together. Instead, I honored a commitment to colleagues, believing I was doing the responsible thing at the time.

That choice—leaving when we needed each other most—became a painful lesson: even a decision that feels responsible in the moment can still be the wrong one.

Though I boarded the plane, part of me never left that meeting. The rejection we faced there lingered, forcing us to look farther—and what we found next would test not only our resolve but our family's closeness.

Choosing Care, Losing Closeness

Choosing residential care for your child isn't merely a decision—it's a reckoning. One shaped by hope, heartbreak, and the fragile trust we place in others.

For us, this choice came with soul-searching, emotional upheaval, and an unwavering commitment to Tyler's best interests.

After considerable exploration, we discovered an organization offering residential school placement for children with severe autism—a place built specifically for students like Tyler.

Our initial visit moved us deeply.

The hallways echoed with laughter—each child distinct, yet all sharing similar challenges. In that moment, we felt both humbled and hopeful.

The educators spoke passionately about their work—their devotion to routines and personalized learning plans, even for basic skills, was reassuring. It was clear the teachers understood autism and knew how to adapt to each child's learning style. The prospect of Tyler being supported by professionals who understood him gave us hope for his future.

Everyone we met seemed confident they could help Tyler learn and thrive. As we concluded our visit, we felt an uneasy mixture of sadness and optimism. Though it was four hours from our home, we wondered if this residential program might be the best choice for our son.

In the days following our visit, we discussed the pros and cons, wrestling with doubt. We tried, half-heartedly, to talk ourselves out of it—but the benefits were undeniable.

Ultimately, we reached a difficult consensus: Tyler belonged in this program.

But the cost was beyond our means, so the final decision hinged on whether our local school system would cover the cost.

Convincing our town to fund the program proved challenging. We presented our case with conviction, emphasizing the positive impact this environment would have on Tyler's development and well-being.

It was a delicate negotiation—we had to advocate for Tyler's needs while acknowledging that the local school, despite its best intentions, wasn't equipped to provide what he required.

Their reluctance pushed us toward legal counsel.

Our lawyer, an expert in disability education law, became our champion, asserting the school's obligation to provide for Tyler.

Despite his strong advocacy, the school's stance was unyielding, convinced of its ability to provide an acceptable educational setting.

When it became clear we were getting nowhere, our lawyer suggested an unorthodox strategy: a meeting with the school superintendent—Tyler in tow.

The plan was to let Tyler explore the superintendent's office freely. Half-joking, our lawyer suggested that if Tyler decided to remove the computer from the desk, we should let him.

It was a calculated risk, intended to underscore Tyler's need for care beyond what the local school could offer.

During the meeting, Tyler moved through the office with the restless energy that defined this phase of his life, touching everything within reach. While Tyler didn't send any computers crashing to the floor, his presence served as a powerful demonstration of the care he would require.

The school conceded.

While I generally dislike resorting to lawyers, in this instance it was necessary—and proved indispensable in advocating Tyler's educational rights.

But now the hard part began for all of us.

The decision to pursue residential care wasn't just about Tyler—it was about all of us. Our marriage, already strained by years of constant vigilance, now faced a new test: four-hour drives, every weekend for the foreseeable future. Our other children would give up their weekends without complaint—a sacrifice we didn't fully appreciate until much later.

We told ourselves we could handle it. Families do hard things.

We were bracing for separation, hoping it would lead to growth. But what we didn't yet understand was that Tyler's world—his rhythms, his instincts, his humor—would continue to shape ours, even from a distance.

Distance changed our routines, but it never dimmed the light of who Tyler was. Seeing him clearly became our new task.

Through Tyler's Eyes

By now, you've met Tyler—the heart and soul of this story.

But beyond that introduction lies a deeper portrait of the young man who continues to shape my life in ways I'm still learning to understand.

Tyler shows kindness to everyone, especially those more vulnerable than himself.

He has a particular affinity for babies—smiling warmly whenever he sees one or hears a cry. When given the chance to interact, he reaches out with a light touch, so gentle it's deeply moving.

Yet his gentle nature also leaves him exposed.

He rarely defends himself—even when he should—and there have been times when others have struck him. This is especially concerning in environments he shares with others who, through no fault of their own, may act aggressively.

Tyler's skills are limited. He will respond to some verbal cues, but the results don't always align with conventional expectations.

He often appears lost in thought, and it's hard to know what he understands. Yet it's clear his mind is frequently at work.

Occasionally, he surprises me—like the times he pulls me toward my car in a crowded lot—a feat that has saved me more than once.

His fascination with Play-Doh is striking—not just the tactile pleasure, but the logo and container themselves.

In the chaos of busy stores, he can spot the Play-Doh symbol from afar. His eyes sharpen, zeroing in on his target with an urgency that seems to say, "There! That's what I want to see!"

His fascination with symbols isn't limited to Play-Doh—he's equally drawn to the iconic golden arches of McDonald's.

Countless times, within sight of a McDonald's, he fixates on the sign with an intensity that suggests he sees something beyond its commercial purpose.

What's intriguing is that while he enjoys McDonald's, he'll sometimes decline my offer to go inside. It's as if the allure lies not just in the food itself, but in the visual appeal of the brand.

Tyler's fascinations might seem surface-level, but his ability to form deep emotional bonds is not. And every now and then, he lets us see just how deep those bonds run.

At the age of twenty-two—a month after my daughter left for college—he showed me exactly how much he cherishes loved ones.

Tyler, who typically remains in his room once settled in for the night, opened his door, and slowly descended the stairs. His eyes carried a weight I hadn't seen before—a deep sorrow, as if something inside him had shifted.

I approached him and gently asked what was wrong.

For a moment he stood in silence, as if wondering how to express himself. He then pointed to a photo of his sister. No words—just a gesture. An aching admission: he missed her deeply.

In that moment, I saw the depth of his feelings in a way I hadn't before. It was a rare glimpse into emotions he carries but can't express.

As a parent, that incident stirred a cascade of questions that I still carry: What else does he feel that I'm missing? What other emotions are waiting for a way to be seen?

That night reminded me his world holds far more than meets the eye—grief, connection, longing. It's in there, but hard to recognize.

But just as he can surprise us with muted sorrow, he can leave us doubled over in laughter. His sense of timing, his literal interpretations, and his unfiltered honesty have created moments so absurd, so perfectly Tyler, that they've become family lore.

So, before we get too comfortable in the solemnity of things, let's take a detour.

The next chapter celebrates the hilarity of raising my son—reminding us that even in silence, humor has its own language.

Humor Without Words

Tyler's humor and keen sense of right and wrong add vibrant dimensions to who he is.

Without words, he's found his own ways to express amusement. And he has a mischievous streak that proves he's tuned into the people around him.

When he sees others laugh, he often joins in—proof that he picks up on social cues and wants to be part of the moment. This shared laughter creates connection, emphasizing his awareness of the joy that laughter brings.

Then there are moments that would make Miss Manners blush. He delights in the kinds of bodily noises most of us pretend didn't happen. Where others might squirm or offer a sheepish apology, he bursts into laughter—pure, unfiltered, contagious.

It's not mischief. Life isn't always meant to be polished. Sometimes, it's meant to be funny.

I find myself laughing too—not at him, but with him. Because Tyler has a way of turning the ordinary into something worth celebrating, even if it leaves the rest of us checking the air behind us.

Tyler's smile surfaces when he's clearly eyeing something off-limits, preparing to reach for it with a glint in his eye. Other times, his smile reveals itself for reasons known only to him.

That mystery adds a delightful unpredictability to his demeanor, as if he's tuned to a private channel of humor—one only he can hear.

His approach to giving kisses is just as unpredictable.

Sometimes he'll give a sweet kiss without hesitation. Other times he refuses—wearing a playful smile, he walks right past, keeping us guessing.

Among the signs Tyler has mastered is the gesture for needing the restroom. At times he will use this sign to break the rules. Knowing this sign prompts an immediate response, he'll flash it to pause an activity he's lost interest in.

Initially, this tactic led to unnecessary bathroom breaks. Now, I question his intent. When he signals the need to use the restroom, I ask if he truly needs to go.

If he does, he repeats the sign earnestly.

If not, an impish grin spreads across his face, and he pivots to his "all done" sign—his subtle confession that I've caught him mid-scheme.

And when signs aren't enough, he improvises with physical presence.

If the television is on and he's decided we've seen enough, he'll slowly rise and plant himself directly in front of the screen—tall, silent, immovable.

No drama. No protest.

Just a perfectly timed, human-shaped blockade. It's his way of saying, "Let's do something else."

At first, this tactic felt like interruption. Now, I see it as an invitation.

Yet laughter has its limits, and behind this humor lies a harder truth.

Far too often signs are missing—expressions are unreadable—cues aren't there.

It's then that a deep helplessness settles in. I find myself wondering: Is he happy? What brings him joy? Is he feeling safe, content?

I search his face for something—anything—that will tell me what words cannot.

It's the ache of not knowing. Not because he won't tell me, but because he can't. I want to be the kind of parent who intuits what his child needs—but the truth is—sometimes I miss it. Despite all I've learned, I get it wrong.

And so I do the only thing I can. Stay close. Show up. Offer comfort. Observe.

And just when we think we understand his humor, Tyler rewrites the rules in ways only he can.

The Candy Game

You've read about heartbreak, marital strain, the challenges of caregiving, and unpredictable humor—but perhaps you're still struggling to picture the young man at the center of all this.

That's fair. Honestly, after thirty-seven years, I'm still not sure I've figured him out.

Tyler is a puzzle I joyfully fail to solve. And just when I think I know his limitations, he teaches me a new lesson—often with impeccable timing and, in this case, candy.

There's a long-standing belief that individuals with Tyler's level of autism have limited ability to learn, adapt, or strategize. But Tyler reminds me otherwise—especially when food is involved.

Over time, I've used his healthy appetite to craft simple games that keep him engaged while encouraging learning. One of our favorites is the "which hand" game. We'd played this game for a long time—long enough that I thought I knew how it always went.

It's simple: I place a small piece of candy—usually an M&M—in one fist. I show him both closed hands and ask, "Which hand, Tyler?"

If he chooses correctly, he wins the candy. If not, we go again until he does. It's light, playful, and over the years, it's been played many times. Usually, he picks a hand at random—hopeful, sometimes amused, mostly indifferent. But one month after his thirty-seventh birthday, during a store visit, the game took an unexpected turn.

Armed with a few M&M's, I said, "Which hand, Tyler?" Like always, I extended both fists, expecting him to choose.

Instead, he paused.

A slow, playful grin crept across his face—the kind that stops me in my tracks. Without hesitation, he extended both of his hands—palm up—one beneath my right fist, one beneath my left.

He wasn't choosing—he was catching.

In that instant, he upended the rules. No more 50/50 chance. No more trying his luck. He'd decoded the pattern, calculated the outcome, and ensured his victory. Candy was coming, regardless of where I'd hidden it.

I couldn't help myself—I laughed. Loudly. Shoppers turned to look, but I didn't care. It was a sign of pure brilliance, and it belonged entirely to him.

What struck me wasn't that he'd found a clever workaround, but how perfectly it captured something larger: My son had been watching. He'd been learning. On his own terms, in his own time, and in a way no textbook could measure.

It took thirty-seven years. It was brilliant.

It was a declaration: *"I know more than you think."*

And that is one of his great strengths. He keeps us curious. He defies definition.

The candy game doesn't define his potential; it only offers a glimpse. Because understanding someone like him isn't about measurement—it's about noticing.

And maybe that's enough.

The question "How much does Tyler really know and what would he say if he could speak?" doesn't have a tidy answer. Still, moments like the M&M game leave me with questions my heart keeps asking. And sometimes, my subconscious joins the conversation.

More than once, I've had dreams in which Tyler is speaking. Not in sentences I could follow—just the unmistakable sound of his voice. Upon hearing his voice, I freeze—startled and awed. Afraid that any response might shatter the miracle. I strategize what to say next, hoping that careful conversation might hold the moment in place.

The dreams—and the emotions they stir—feel deeply real. But they are, of course—dreams. They're reflections of my own longing—for his comfort, for clearer connection, for access to the full person I've only known through gestures, glances, and presence.

What's most telling is this: in all my years with Tyler, this is the only dream I've had about him. No adventures. No milestones. Just speech. And it is through this speech that I hope to understand more of who he is. To uncover what makes him happy.

Moments like the candy game reveal how far he has come—and how much he has always understood. But the reason that moment matters so deeply is rooted in the years that came before.

Not the beginning of our story, but the stretch of time when uncertainty ruled our days, and when a four-hour drive—and the promise attached to it—shaped everything.

Four Hours and a Promise

The school where Tyler would be living was ideal in many ways: thoughtful, well-equipped, tailored for children with severe autism.

But it was in a seaside vacation community—four hours away.

And that changed everything.

We told ourselves we'd visit every weekend.

We meant it.

But even before the first visit, that promise grew heavier. The question wasn't *"Will we go?"*—it was *"How will we make it work?"*

Relocating closer to the school was tempting—it would simplify the logistics, soften the distance.

But reality pulled us back. What about the rest of our family—friends, teachers, the sense of home we'd built? Disrupting that would ripple far beyond geography.

There was also my job—stable, secure, and necessary. At a time when Tyler was stepping into something unfamiliar, risking more disruption felt reckless.

Convenience wasn't the goal. Holding our family together while still giving him what he needed was.

So we stayed. And staying exposed the true impact of distance.

Weekend housing near the school was scarce. Hotels were expensive. A second home, out of reach. Every solution felt partial, strained, or impossible.

That first weekend hadn't even arrived, yet I already felt the strain. I pictured the drive—soda in hand, kids half-asleep, the road stretching endlessly ahead. Each of us wondering—*Was this the best decision?*

Our promise to visit wasn't just a commitment—it was the thread holding our connection together, week after week.

And now, we were about to learn something hard: It wasn't simply about arriving. It was also about letting go—even when every part of you wants to hold on.

The First Goodbye

The first time we left Tyler at his new school, a strange quiet wrapped around us. Not because we didn't feel—but because we felt too much. The goodbye wasn't dramatic. He stood beside his new teacher, calm and unreadable. But inside, something cracked.

That moment came later. First came moving day.

Moving day had arrived, and with it came the uneasy reckoning: Tyler's new home would reshape everything, including the world of his siblings.

At an age when weekends were sacred—filled with playdates, birthday parties, and slow mornings—they faced eight hours in the car, every weekend.

The weight of that sacrifice was real.

In hindsight, we didn't discuss this upheaval in their lives with the depth it deserved. It marked the beginning of sacrifices we didn't yet understand.

Weeks before move-in day, a friend of Tyler's mother offered us a lifeline: the use of her vacation home during our initial visits. It was a gift that eased more than logistics—it softened our stress, giving us space to breathe.

Our first weekend trip opened a new chapter.

We told Tyler he'd be living with new friends, a concept that floated past him. For our other children, we painted the visits with promise: fun activities, favorite restaurants, and the comfort of the vacation house.

Upon arriving, the school's management and staff gave us a warm welcome, reassuring us that we had made the right choice.

During our visit, the atmosphere was surprisingly light, and as conversations unfolded, we grew more confident this residential school could provide exceptional care.

Despite our growing confidence, reluctance surfaced. For the first time, we were preparing to leave Tyler in the care of new teachers and caregivers. Our hesitation wasn't doubt—it was responsibility.

As we prepared to leave for the first time, I glanced back at Tyler. His face gave nothing away—no smile, no frown, no sign that he understood what was happening.

Blankness was worse than tears. Crying can be comforted. Silence cannot.

I wanted to freeze the moment, to beg for just one clue, one sign, that told me he was okay. Instead, all I had was the sound of my own shoes on the hallway floor as we walked away.

I turned back to look—once, briefly.

Heading to our car without him, the emotions overwhelmed me. Any sense that we'd made the right decision vanished. Doubt and anxiety took hold.

How could we do this?

Was my son feeling abandoned?

Was sending Tyler to this residential school an act of cowardice, a surrender of the most significant responsibility one could assume—being a parent?

I hesitated as I touched the handle of the car door.

The drive home was muted.

It wasn't distance. It was the emotional fallout of choosing something hard in the name of doing what we believed was right.

What I didn't understand yet was that this was the start of a much harder road.

Adaptation wasn't a choice. It became our family's second language.

Finding Our Rhythm Apart

Over the next several years, our family settled into a routine—born of necessity but shaped by love.

Every Friday afternoon, we packed up and made the drive, gathering as a family to spend the weekend with Tyler.

Shortly after Tyler settled into his new school, a small financial windfall arrived—perfectly timed. It came from the business trip I'd taken the day of Tyler's rejection—the trip I shouldn't have prioritized (see "The Door That Stayed Closed").

The company I worked for had been acquired, and during that trip, I negotiated a bonus that gave us the means to make a down payment and secure a mortgage on a second home, a mere few miles from his school.

I still regret choosing that trip over being home when it mattered most. But from it came this: the chance to put down roots near Tyler's new world.

We called it "Tyler's weekend home." It became the place where guilt and grace shared a roof.

The conflict between work and family remained an undertow.

Money couldn't cure autism, buy happiness, or replace the irreplaceable—the goodnight kisses, the connection children crave.

But in this case, it offered something rare: a small salvation.

The transition—at least for Tyler—was smooth. He adapted to this new school more easily than any of us.

Within the first few months, the benefits of his new learning environment began to show: behavioral challenges softened, toilet training clicked, and limited sign language began to take shape.

These changes, however small, were transformative—providing essential skills previously out of reach.

The emotional rollercoaster of placing Tyler in a residential school began to settle.

This path wasn't chosen because it was easy. It was right—for Tyler, for us, for the equilibrium our family was learning to protect.

Each weekend—the drive—the restaurants—the return—we watched as he settled into himself.

He gained skills, yes—but more than that, he gained calm. It was as if the Energizer Bunny that once fueled chaos had been tamed—a human finally finding his rhythm.

For the first time in a long while, his world felt steady.

The question was, did ours?

Trying Anyway

State regulations ensured Tyler's education would be funded through age twenty-two, allowing him to remain in the residential school that had become his haven.

Knowing that he would continue receiving tailored educational resources and care through early adulthood gave us a measure of relief.

Amid so many unknowns, this one certainty offered us something rare: comfort.

Before his tenth birthday, progress plateaued. Therapists introduced communication boards and job-skills training—nothing stuck. He took steps forward, but they led nowhere meaningful.

We turned our focus to finding new activities that might bring joy and a sense of accomplishment.

Some led to triumph. Others remained beyond reach.

One success arrived through bicycle rides. On our tandem bike—Tyler in back, me in front—we'd cover more than ten miles at a stretch.

It wasn't just exercise; it felt like a fleeting glimpse of what he might one day be capable of.

During these rides, Tyler's mother joined in, turning the experience into a humorous game of vocal tag.

Picture this: a tandem bike gliding down the path, two riders in sync, his mother and our other two children trailing behind.

But her role wasn't just pedaling—she provided a constant vocal soundtrack.

As the wind whipped by, her voice called out: "Tyler, hold on!"

It became a rhythmic chant, part instruction, part comedy.

The rides weren't always easy; they came with constant reminders and corrections. But Tyler leaned into the thrill, letting go of the handlebars as he coasted down the path—carefree, curious, defiant.

Just as biking opened one door, skiing released another.

Skilled volunteers guided Tyler down the snow-covered slopes, tethered by two ropes, navigating the twists and turns of the mountainous descent—something we never could have imagined. It was another activity we could all share as a family.

Though short-lived, these were meaningful wins.

His loss of interest in biking was hard to explain—and harder to accept. Before long, he lost interest in skiing too. We suspected the frigid winter conditions made skiing unpleasant, but we couldn't know for sure.

These successes, brief and infrequent, held immense significance—their rarity made them precious.

Then came moments that reminded us how fragile that balance was.

The scene: a Mother's Day brunch at a grand hotel with a bustling restaurant filled with patrons.

As we tried to celebrate his mother, Tyler's restlessness prompted me—as it often did—to take him for a brief walk through the hotel corridors.

That innocent walk took an unexpected turn.

Reaching out without hesitation, Tyler pulled the fire alarm.

In an instant, the ambiance shifted—from casual enjoyment to full-blown chaos.

Buffet lines scattered. The near-full ballroom emptied. Scrambled eggs sat cooling, untouched, and lonely.

In retrospect, such incidents may evoke laughter—but in the moment—they are both stressful and embarrassing.

Our days with Tyler were unpredictable. He never followed a chart or checklist.

Normal life was rarely perfect and often not easy. I didn't know it yet, but I had to start seeing things differently.

Seeing differently meant not only watching Tyler adapt, but accepting him as he was—and accepting what that meant for the rest of us.

Accepting, Finally

We visited Tyler more than two hundred and fifty times in those first five years of residential care, but rarely spoke about what it was costing us.

Yet, the slight smile on Tyler's face as we arrived always made the trip worthwhile.

The impact on our other children appeared minimal—though it was hard to tell. The toll on our marriage was anything but minimal.

Everyday joy had faded from our partnership. What remained was planning, caregiving, and the constant grind of survival.

Alone time became a luxury we couldn't afford. Our constant absence on weekends eroded the outside friendships and lightness a marriage should bring.

During this period, our disagreements became more frequent as the cracks in our marriage widened.

We found it easier not to talk—because talking led nowhere.

Then, I lost my job.

The structure I had relied on—professionally and emotionally—vanished overnight. Suddenly, there was no place to go each day, no rhythm to steady the heaviness of everything else unraveling.

Being without a job added one more thing I couldn't control—when everything else felt unsteady. Unemployed and home all day, the tension increased. We came to a hard truth: we needed a break from our marriage.

I moved into a hotel. The separation was brief.

The events of 9/11 brought a stark realization of the importance of family—prompting me to return home. We needed to make a greater effort to coexist, for the sake of our children and ourselves.

The commitment to peace lasted for a while but ultimately proved unsustainable. Living apart became a recurring theme.

As Tyler's intellectual progression plateaued, the reality set in—this would be his life—he would always need 24/7 care.

Clarity for me came during Tyler's fourteenth year.

While I struggled, I marveled at Tyler's acceptance of his fate. Here was a child entirely dependent on others, seemingly content in his surroundings—pushing forward despite limitations.

Most of us cannot understand what that level of dependence means. Someone tells Tyler when to get up, even if he doesn't feel up to it. He never gets a day off.

He's told when to eat and what to eat. He doesn't get to determine what brings joy to his life—we guess and hope it works. What he wears, how his hair is cut, the soap and shampoo he uses—he has no choice.

And yet he accepts it. Not with resignation, but with a quiet grace I'm still learning from.

Watching him navigate a life with no autonomy—and his ability to still find moments of contentment—forced me to a realization: I had two choices. I could continue to dwell in grief over what would never be, or I could embrace what was.

I chose the latter.

This shift has guided me for more than twenty years.

Still, deep down, sorrow remains.

A poignant memory: a play in New York City that depicted the helplessness of loving someone with profound disabilities.

On stage, a caregiver faced an impossible truth: love, no matter how complete, couldn't change the world's apathy toward someone who was different. I watched him—the caregiver—reckon with that reality, and every fear I'd carried about Tyler's future surfaced at once. The weight of protection. The limits of devotion. The question that haunts every parent like me: *Who will care when I can't?*

As the actors moved through their story, I felt a pressure rising in my chest. It wasn't dramatic—just a slow, steady breaking I couldn't stop.

Leaving the theater, I crossed the street. I collapsed onto a bench and wept—long, loud, and uncontrollably. It wasn't just grief—it was the release of years spent holding it all together.

It was embarrassing, yes—but more than that, it was liberating.

I don't expect sorrow to leave. I've just stopped letting it decide how the day unfolds—most of the time.

In the exchanges between us—in Tyler's loving eyes, his engaging smile—I find what grief cannot touch.

I would be lying if I said it was easy.

The same year I learned to accept Tyler's reality, I had to accept another: our marriage was ending. We stopped living together when Tyler was fifteen. The divorce was finalized two years later.

Many couples in our situation don't make it. I once believed we'd be the exception. We weren't. Neither of us wanted it to end, but staying together was no longer in anyone's best interest. What stuck with us wasn't anger, but the profound grief of something we couldn't hold together.

We didn't break because of Tyler. We broke trying not to fail him.

Less Space, Same Love

After the divorce, everything shifted—logistics, routines, even the shape of home itself.

The divorce agreement required me to remain in our hometown, a stipulation crucial for keeping educational funding.

The urgency to secure a new residence left me with few choices. Ultimately, I moved from the family home to a modestly furnished one-bedroom apartment above a two-car garage.

It wasn't much—just an apartment above a garage. But it was mine. And more importantly, it kept the financial support intact.

The space was modest. The intention was fierce.

Without notice, town authorities questioned my residency, suspecting I had signed the lease to safeguard Tyler's educational funding with no intent of residing in this "above-the-garage" space.

When police officers arrived to verify I lived there, I welcomed them in without hesitation. Upon questioning, I said, "Yes, I live here," and one officer gave the place a slow once-over before offering a small, almost apologetic smile.

Dirty laundry, dishes in the sink, food on the stove—me at the desk. It was proof enough.

They left quickly, carrying with them a glimpse of what divorce had thrust upon me.

Tyler's mom and I maintained a collaborative approach, setting aside personal differences to ensure the best for our family. Alternating weekends became a practical solution, offering each of us a reprieve.

My square footage had shrunk—but not my commitment.

The Pain We Can't See

Caring for someone who cannot speak means learning to read pain in silence.

One incident involved Tyler being rushed to the hospital with a ruptured appendix. By the time complications arose, the infection had spread to peritonitis—a life-threatening condition.

Days of agony had been masked—sometimes even with laughter.

My first instinct was fury—how could this have gone unnoticed? But beneath the anger was something else—an understanding of how impossible diagnosis can be when pain has no words.

Another medical event unfolded in the form of dental surgery. The surgery itself was uneventful. Little did I know the aftermath would turn my home into a quirky comedy that suddenly veered into horror.

After surgery, Tyler endured forty-eight hours of intermittent bleeding.

I became a one-man cleanup crew—armed with towels and tissues, determined to shield every couch and carpet. He was calm through it all, while I staged a frantic ballet around him.

In the end, it became less horror show, more family lore—something we still laugh about today.

Beyond those dramatic episodes, Tyler has, for the most part, enjoyed good health. Minor medical events—dental visits, blood draws, checkups—revealed his surprising cooperation.

The mystery of what goes on inside his mind persists.

I cautiously assume he comprehends more than we realize—and I'm convinced he has a keen awareness of those who offer their help.

Still, the concern remains: what if a serious illness goes undetected? How do we recognize signs of pain or discomfort when the individual cannot verbalize them?

During visits, we conduct health checks. Sometimes I want to examine every inch of his body with a magnifying glass—then I stop myself.

I should note that Tyler's mother, a nurse practitioner, has been instrumental in safeguarding his health. Her clinical insight and unwavering advocacy ensure he receives the best possible care.

Tyler's body is still a mystery—silent in suffering, unpredictable in recovery, surprisingly cooperative in moments that should overwhelm him.

With him, medical knowledge is not always enough. Humility is required. The kind that accepts not having every answer. The kind that keeps arriving with tissues, towels, and hope.

Tyler doesn't tell me when he's in pain. Sometimes, I don't tell anyone when I am either. We both carry things in silence.

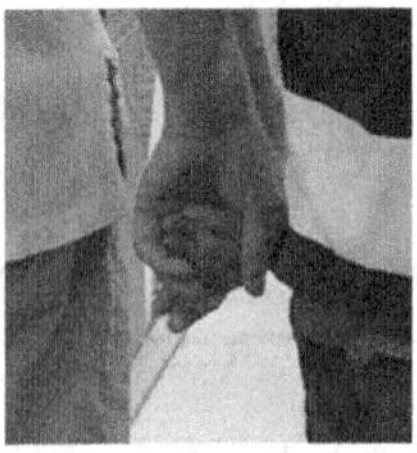

But in those moments—when he reaches for my hand, when I catch his gaze—I remember: we're not meant to carry it alone.

With Us, Not Between Us

Living alone nudged a question to the surface: "Could I find someone who wouldn't just accept my world, but embrace it?"

With a good deal of hesitation, I dipped my toes into dating. And if dating in your fifties teaches you anything, it's that everyone carries some baggage.

After several first dates—and no second ones—I realized combining two lives shaped by kids, divorces, and caregiving wasn't going to be easy.

I knew my situation clearly. Anyone who came into my world would need to be flexible and compassionate. Tyler's needs would sometimes take precedence—without apology. And unfortunately, that kind of partner doesn't appear often.

But then, out of nowhere, I met someone extraordinary. She embraced the contours of my complicated world without hesitation. She instantly connected with my kids and Tyler in ways that felt natural, even serendipitous.

Her art pulled me into conversations I never would've started on my own; my sports banter gave her a reason to cheer when the Patriots won a Super Bowl. Somehow, it worked.

For the past nineteen years, she's been my confidant, my companion, and my steadying force in the chaos of everyday life.

And Tyler? Well, he had his own way of vetting newcomers.

The first time she met him, we were sitting together on the couch speaking as Tyler paced nearby. He moved back and forth with a familiar rhythm, sneaking a peek at us as he passed—casually at first, then more intently.

Then, without warning, Tyler walked over and plopped himself firmly between the two of us, claiming the middle cushion with unmistakable conviction.

It was more than a seating preference—it was a message. He didn't rely on words to express how he felt, but his presence spoke volumes: "Be careful. Don't come between me and my dad."

To her credit, she didn't flinch. She offered him a warm smile, nodded, and scooted over without resistance. Tyler sat there a bit longer, satisfied.

He had drawn the boundary, and she had respected it. No power struggle, no confusion. Just mutual acceptance, spoken without words.

That small moment—wedged between couch cushions—marked a shift. It wasn't dramatic or ceremonial—but it mattered. Tyler had offered his first test, and she had passed.

The complexities of caregiving haven't magically been resolved. The routines, the worries, the mental juggling act—they're all still here. The road remains unpredictable.

However, in this new partnership, I've found something unexpected: not fewer complications—but fewer lonely ones.

She didn't try to fix things; she became a trusted co-pilot.

Tyler didn't need her to decode him. I didn't need her to carry the responsibility.

We just needed someone who saw us clearly—and chose to stay.

Finding Home Again and Again

Stability matters. For individuals with autism, it's more than comfort—it's survival. But stability isn't always possible.

Between ages nineteen and twenty-five, Tyler experienced three major moves. Three times, everything he knew changed.

The first came when his residential school closed—a school he started at the age of five. Tyler had lived there for fourteen years—longer than most children spend in their childhood homes.

I shared the news with him during our weekend visit, knowing he would not understand.

His current school was in a charming seaside village. His bedroom had a view of a golf course and the ocean. The new school was over an hour away from the home we'd purchased just to be near Tyler. It was also in a more urban setting—just a different rhythm, one Tyler hadn't known before.

The irony was bitter: we'd bought a house near his school, and now he was moving even farther away.

We kept the house, but our weekend ritual—once a familiar route to a place we knew well—became a longer journey with a stop at somewhere unfamiliar.

For Tyler, everything changed—his room, his caregivers, the routines that had once grounded him. When he first entered the new school, it was hard to tell if he was exploring or searching for something that wasn't there.

We held our breath. Would he sleep through the night? Would the new staff understand him?

Tyler surprised us. He explored the new space cautiously, then settled in. New caregivers learned his ways—how he signals when he's ready for bed, how he shows affection, how he makes his needs known without words.

It wasn't easy, but he adapted. And somehow, in this new place, the right people found him. Caregivers who saw past his limitations to who he truly was.

As Tyler entered his twenty-first year, another transition loomed. His time in the school environment would soon be ending. Uncertainty lingered: Where would he live next? Would it be safe? Would it feel like home?

Fortunately, the organization behind Tyler's school also ran group homes for adults with disabilities.

Shortly before Tyler turned twenty-two, a spot opened in one of the homes. This was his second major move—from the structured school environment to a group home setting.

Naturally, concerns surfaced—about the new living arrangement, the risk of regression, and whether the environment would truly support him.

The transition brought significant changes to Tyler's daily life. A dayhab program was found—offering weekday care, community-based activities, and job placement for those who could pursue it. Tyler wasn't among them.

What mattered more to him was the bus ride—he loved watching the world go by, each day a new adventure.

Though the program lacked the personalized education of his residential school, it fostered new friendships and brought a welcome stability to his life.

What made these changes bearable were the caregivers—people who connected with Tyler, communicated with us, and truly saw him.

We began to hope this was it—that Tyler had found his home.

Just as he started recognizing faces and learning the house rules, another notification arrived. His new group home was closing. Another move. Another adjustment.

This third move took him to a different town. Different streets on our weekend drives. Different stores for his balloons. Different people learning his habits, his preferences, and that his silence isn't emptiness.

Once again, we held our breath. Once again, Tyler had to adapt.

Three homes in six years. Each time, we wondered: Will this be the one that lasts?

Each time, Tyler proved he was stronger than we knew. He'd explore each new space with the same cautious curiosity, learning unfamiliar faces, new routines, new sounds, and smells.

And each time, caregivers emerged who didn't just care for Tyler—they cared about him.

They learned his language. They celebrated when he placed his hand in theirs. They understood that his bottle cap ritual wasn't odd—it was essential. They saw him.

It's these caregivers—appearing in each new place like guardians—who made the instability bearable. They didn't let Tyler become lost in the shuffle of closures and relocations. They let him be Tyler, not a diagnosis.

And finally, mercifully, the third place held.

The moves stopped. The caregivers stayed. The routines that Tyler needed—and that we needed for him—took root.

For a parent, knowing that someone truly sees your child, understands them, advocates for them when you're not there—that means everything.

Tyler's world may have shifted beneath him three times in six years, but through it all, he found his footing. With every move, Tyler kept finding home again and again—not in places, but in people who chose to see him—day after day.

That's what carried him through. That's what carries him still.

Care in Crisis

The world unraveled with the arrival of COVID.

Tyler's group home, like so many others, imposed strict isolation. Residents who had contact with anyone outside their immediate circle—that meant us—were barred from returning. Our weekend visits, the ritual we'd kept for years, were suddenly forbidden.

We faced a brutal choice: stay away or bring him home.

We had made a promise, so we chose home.

I rearranged my work schedule to care for him three days a week. His mom took the other four. It wasn't easy. But it gave us something rare—uninterrupted time with Tyler, while the rest of the world lived in isolation.

COVID's impact reached far beyond our home. The world had shut down.

Tyler thrives on being out in the world. Our days revolve around mall visits, lunch at restaurants, and the occasional stop for a hot fudge sundae. All of it vanished.

Tyler used to lead me through the mall, hand in mine, navigating the familiar route—food court, balloon store, a loop past the fountain.

During COVID, we sometimes drove to the closed mall parking lot. He'd look at the locked doors, then back at me. No words. Just the question in his eyes: Why not today?

I'd sit there with him for a moment, wishing I had an answer that made sense to either of us. Even finding a new balloon—his weekend ritual and source of joy—was suddenly out of reach.

With our usual destinations closed, filling the day became a challenge.

Each Saturday during COVID, Tyler walked to the hallway and returned with his shoes. Expectantly, he would place them in my hand.

It was his signal—clear as any spoken word. *Time to go. Ready for our weekend adventure.*

I'd look at the shoes, then at Tyler's expectant face. For seventeen years, this gesture had meant the same thing: mall visits, restaurants, grocery stores, the familiar rhythm we had established.

"Tyler," I'd say gently, "there's nowhere to go today."

I would set the shoes down and try to explain what couldn't be explained—or understood.

"The mall is closed. Most restaurants are closed. Everything is closed."

But Tyler would move to the front door, waiting.

By noon, I surrendered. We couldn't stay inside—his restlessness was mounting, and truthfully, so was mine. We'd find a restaurant offering takeout and place our order.

Twenty minutes later, we'd sit in my car in their parking lot with containers of food balanced on our laps. Tyler eating his chicken fingers methodically, occasionally glancing toward the restaurant's locked front door as if waiting for it to open and invite us in.

It wasn't the weekend he expected—or the one I'd hoped for. But watching him adapt to this strange new reality—eating lunch in a car because the world had changed overnight—I realized we were both learning the same hard lesson.

Sometimes the only choice is to improvise—to do the best you can.

Beyond disrupting routines, the pandemic exposed the fragility of every system we relied on.

Group homes and dayhab programs faced a staffing collapse. Some caregivers left for higher-paying jobs. Others left altogether. The result wasn't theoretical—it was Tyler losing his day program for over a year.

No outings. No structure. Just long days at home, waiting for something to return.

While small businesses and airlines received billions in support, the people who cared for Tyler—who bathed him, taught him, kept him safe—were left behind.

And for families like ours, the fallout hurt.

Caregivers are the backbone of disability support. They show up—day after day—with patience, grit, and grace. They deserve more than praise. They deserve pay that reflects their worth. Policies that protect their future. Respect that isn't conditional.

As an advocate, watching their neglect was infuriating. As a parent, it was personal.

We did what we could. We adjusted our lives, made the best decisions possible—and the world kept its distance.

But beneath every decision was fear: How do we protect his future when the systems created to support him are so fragile—and our time with him so achingly finite?

The answer, I've learned, isn't found in systems alone. It's found in the caregivers who show up—the ones who see Tyler, who learn his language, who treat him with dignity even when no one is watching. They are the bridge between our fear and his future. They are why we can keep showing up, even when the systems feel fragile.

They deserve more than our gratitude. They deserve our support, our advocacy, and recognition that their work holds families like ours together.

The Cost of Showing Up

Raising a child with significant support needs comes with financial realities—not complaints, just truths.

We've been fortunate in our careers, allowing us to provide for Tyler's needs. Yet the question remained: *How much is enough?* In other words, what financial reserve is needed to ensure proper care after we're gone?

Seeking clarity, I asked aloud—then searched for answers: *What does "enough" actually look like?*

The responses pointed to a range of considerations, each urging a personalized approach.

Despite valuable input, no one could offer a number. There is no definitive answer to the "How much is enough" question.

What if it's never enough?

That fear was present with every paycheck, every choice, every plan for the future. It turned math into something heavier—an accounting of guilt as much as dollars.

This uncertainty shaped my choices. It led to cautious spending and influenced how I navigated through my professional life. There were days when the math felt less about the numbers and more about concern: over whether I'd left enough margin, enough insurance, enough calm in a storm I might not be there to weather.

At sixty-two, I lost my job. The pressure to secure Tyler's future pushed me into a less-than-ideal position. The commute to the "Tyler house"—ten hours on a good day. It wasn't fulfillment; it was fear.

When that job ended, I flirted with the idea of retiring. But the old question came back: How much is enough? A two-hour consulting gig somehow became four years of full-time work.

Tyler's world has added costs—a second home kept for twenty-six years, cars worn down by long commutes, even a new bathtub installed for comfort.

While money will never eliminate the impact of autism, having resources allows for decisions that have enhanced the quality of Tyler's existence.

For many families, navigating the financial intricacies of raising a child with disabilities demands meticulous planning, adaptability, and sacrifice.

I've yet to fully accept that there's no perfect definition of "enough." But each mile traveled, each moment of weighing what matters most, and each dollar spent with Tyler's well-being in mind, brings me closer to believing I gave all I could.

If the numbers never quite add up, that's okay—I think.

For years, I carried the pressure to leave enough behind for him. Only later did I understand that what mattered most to Tyler wasn't the future I was trying to secure, but the presence I was already giving him.

And once I finally retired, showing up became much easier.

Closer Than Ever

Retiring and moving closer to Tyler marked a meaningful turning point—one shaped by years of distance, planning, and the quiet pull of presence.

The "Tyler house," which I kept after our divorce, had long been a haven for weekend visits, but it wasn't suited for permanent living.

So began the search for a new home—one that could meet the evolving needs of our family and honor our current way of living.

Finding a home where Tyler could roam free—and make messes without worry—was essential. We needed a space built for safety but designed for us: a forgiving environment where comfort and self-expression could live side by side.

We weighed everything from condominiums to custom builds, but each option fell short—too impractical, too stressful, too far from what we truly needed.

One evening, after a full day of activities, I started my daily house-hunting online. After endless searches through multiple towns, a property caught my eye. A sprawling ranch with a two-bedroom in-law suite.

My first reaction wasn't excitement, but something about the house whispered, *At least come look.*

Skeptical, I visited the vacant property with Tyler the following day. Walking the grounds and peering through windows, we were intrigued.

Still curious, we returned the next day for a closer look.

Despite focusing our search on properties with antique charm, something about this place felt right. So, I shared the listing with my wife, who agreed to a viewing with a realtor.

While the home may not have been what we initially looked for, the layout showed promise.

What hadn't been part of our criteria—the plot of land with its beautiful trees and shrubbery—became a central selling point. We fell for the land more than the walls—and that shift told us what really mattered: room to breathe, and space for Tyler.

We bought this home.

For more than two decades, every visit with Tyler ended in the same house, the same bedroom. Moving meant rewriting that ritual.

As we prepared to move into our new home, I tried to get him excited about the adventure, knowing he couldn't grasp these reassuring words.

Our first day in this new space was uneventful. He explored his new surroundings with interest and caution.

As bedtime arrived, I sensed apprehension. It quickly became clear he was not ready to spend the night alone in this new, untested bedroom.

Tyler didn't resist, but he didn't let go.

His eyes spoke: "Will you stay while I settle in?"

Over the course of three hours, I sat quietly with him in his bed, holding his hand. Each time I tried to leave, he pulled me back with a vigor that said, "I am not quite ready." I wasn't tired; I was simply present, holding on until he didn't need me to anymore.

Finally, without prompting, he laid down and gently pushed me away—his usual way of letting me know he was ready to be alone. I hugged him and left the room.

He slept through the night.

From that point on, he returned without worry to his new bedroom.

Purchasing this home is a choice we've never regretted. It shows how the needs of a child with disabilities can reshape decisions—but not necessarily force compromise.

The home's proximity to Tyler's group home, a mere fifteen-minute commute, was a significant win. Over twenty-six years, I trekked more than four hundred thousand miles—enough to circle the earth sixteen times—just to see my son.

For sixteen of those years, I passed through a staffed toll booth. The drive became so automatic that many times I didn't remember paying the toll. My hand would extend the money, the gate would lift, and I'd be through—muscle memory replacing conscious thought.

What was once hours and highways became minutes and side streets.

For the first time in decades, I lived close enough to feel peace in the distance.

Entering this new chapter didn't erase the past—it honored it. Every mile and every goodbye that took place in the "Tyler house" wove itself into the foundation of this new space.

It wasn't just a move—it was a soft landing.

Though the walls were new, the purpose remained: to give Tyler space to be fully himself, and our family a home built around acceptance—not architecture.

Joy, One Twist at a Time

Tyler's world is stitched together by joy—quiet, repetitive, sensory joy.

Early on, he found solace in opening and closing doors—a calming activity that hinted at the repetitive patterns that would come to define many of his preferred pastimes. We used to joke he was destined to become a doorman at a high-end hotel.

Over the years, one activity has remained steadfast: his bottle and cap. Each morning, without fail, he seeks this familiar object, engaging in the calming motion of twisting the cap on and off.

Despite my efforts to introduce alternative sensory items—many of which now sit untouched in a chest at home—he returns, without hesitation, to his reliable bottle.

In its simplicity, it brings him peace. It's the first twist of happiness in a day that will hold many.

Food is another steady source of happiness. Tyler isn't especially fussy, but his face lights up when a favorite meal appears.

Food court visits often bloom into moments of expression. Pointing to his meal of choice is part of the visit—a gesture that speaks louder than words.

But at times, that gesture gets interrupted.

A nearby bottle with cap catches his eye—he points, I misread the signal, and he ends up with an unintentional lunch.

There's a flicker of frustration, of course. But later, we laugh. Because joy, like lunch, sometimes arrives by accident.

Finding activities continues to be a delicate dance of trial, error, and the occasional stroke of luck. He gravitates toward anything repetitive: sitting in a tub, filling and emptying buckets of water, or exploring objects that can be opened and closed.

A double kayak outing, initially met with hesitation, turned into a highlight when Tyler brought his bottle along—using it to scoop and pour water—transforming a simple paddle into an engaging sensory experience.

Kayaking with my son is part adventure, part negotiation—with Tyler's beloved bottle, his sensory sea creature, always in tow.

The key to introducing new experiences has often meant pairing them with things he enjoys.

Movie theaters, once off-limits due to his restlessness, became manageable with popcorn.

These creative workarounds don't just open doors—they build connections and memories.

During one restaurant outing, live music caught our attention, and we watched Tyler gently rock to the beat. As I observed, I wondered if this was one of those rare breakthroughs.

As we contemplated dessert, it became clear the steady beat of rock music was soon to be added to his daily activities.

That moment revealed a new passion. From then on, music—especially Guns N' Roses, his favorite—became part of his routine. "Sweet Child O' Mine," a song we once sang to him as a baby, now plays as he settles in for breakfast.

His connection to "Sweet Child O' Mine" is proof that, even when memories appear buried, they're never lost.

Tyler's joys are his own. But the way we share them—that's where our weekends begin.

Weekends, Carried by Routine

Weekends follow a repeated schedule, shaped by the joys Tyler carries into them.

I spend time planning activities, knowing that while grocery runs may not be essential, they offer comfort—small outings that lend structure and connection to our days.

I prefer to be alone with Tyler. This is his time—and mine. The routines we've built work because they're ours, refined over hundreds of weekends. I don't have to explain why we're visiting the same balloon store again or worry that the repetition feels boring to someone else. Tyler and I understand each other. That's enough.

Mall visits are one of those routines.

Tyler enjoys being around people. While walking through the mall's crowded hallways, he will hold my hand. It's a subtle expression of safety and connection.

And, as you may expect, my holding hands with a thirty-seven-year-old man in public elicits myriad reactions from a society that does not always accept what is different.

Some stare. Many look away.

I hold his hand anyway—because love doesn't flinch, and connection doesn't ask for permission.

More than offsetting the judgmental stares are the times we connect with others who share a similar experience.

Encounters with fellow parents of children with disabilities bring an unspoken connection, a quiet acknowledgment of the emotional toll and joys that come with having someone special in your life.

Occasionally, someone will call out from across the mall—"Hello Tyler!"—and we're reminded of how many people have come to know and care about him through his group home, his dayhab program, or his place in the community.

Then there is the balloon.

Tyler has long enjoyed the sound and feel of helium balloons—the way they bounce when tapped, the slight resistance they offer, the way they hover just out of reach before bobbing back down. It's a sensory experience that never fades.

Each weekend begins the same way: a trip to his chosen store for a fresh balloon. Not just any balloon—his favorite, chosen with care.

By now, our visits are so familiar that the moment we walk through the door, the same employee springs into action. He heads straight for the helium tank, smiling as he begins preparing Tyler's balloon—no words needed.

It's hard to say who enjoys our visits more: Tyler, full of anticipation, or the cashier, who beams as if he's handing over a small piece of magic.

It's another reminder that his world isn't built by therapies alone—it's built by people—the kind of people who, knowingly or not, add their own twist of happiness to his life.

A balloon may seem trivial, but in this exchange it becomes something greater: a sign that he is seen, understood, honored.

At home, our time is filled with music, preparing meals, and solving puzzles—or rather, *one puzzle.*

Much like his bottle, Tyler will only engage with one puzzle, *Toy Story*. Each piece he places is a celebration, a small victory in a world that doesn't always feel accessible to him.

His interests and abilities are limited, and that shapes our days. Even the most well-planned schedule has its limits.

Sometimes I glance at the clock—not wishing our time away, but worn out from always thinking two steps ahead.

And yet, it's in those small victories—like a puzzle piece placed with care—that I find renewal, a connection, no complexity needed.

After an outing, Tyler expects dinner within the hour—then bath, puzzle time, and bed.

If we return early, he'll sign for dinner repeatedly—even if it's barely 3 p.m.—eager to continue with the rhythm of his evening.

Staying on schedule brings him peace, and for both of us, following it has become second nature.

His preferences may seem small to some, but they are his anchors.

And isn't that what we all look for? Something known. Something that feels good. Something that makes us feel safe.

As the weekend winds down and we begin the drive back to his group home, a noticeable shift occurs. Seated behind me, Tyler watches the road closely, following the turns that lead to the familiar street he now calls home. His sense of direction is remarkable, and his awareness of what's happening—even without words—is clear.

As we say goodbye, both of us navigate the distance in our own way.

His hand no longer rests in mine, but its imprint remains—a reminder that joy lives in what's known, not just what's new.

And as I drive home, planning the next balloon, the next puzzle, the next twist that starts his day, I realize again: this life may not be typical, but it is treasured.

And joy, for us, is never ordinary—it arrives one twist at a time, just like the cap on his bottle each morning.

What Might Have Been, What Is

My lifelong commitment to Tyler wasn't a conscious decision—it just happened, growing in the quiet resolve of showing up again and again.

Sometimes I wonder—not out of rejection, but in search of understanding—what autism has asked of all of us. Yet even entertaining that thought feels disloyal, as if I'm wishing away a part of him.

Autism shaped everything—our marriage, our weekends, our finances, our retirement plans.

My other children gave up typical weekends for road trips. They never voiced regret. *They should know they were never second.* Just silent heroes in a story that asked more of them than most.

While my retirement didn't unfold as planned, my life has been rich with rewards and lessons—a path I walk with gratitude.

What I still struggle to accept is that Tyler will never achieve independence.

One afternoon, while scanning the news, a headline appeared: "Autistic Man Starves to Death." Reading it sent a shockwave through my soul—a fear of what might happen when we are no longer here to safeguard Tyler's well-being.

Staying alive isn't just about me anymore. It's about Tyler.

The image of him reaching for my hand—only to find it absent—becomes a poignant reminder of the fragility of our existence.

Our good health benefits Tyler. Tyler's mom and I promised we'd visit Tyler every weekend (*see* "Four Hours and a Promise"). It's been close to seventeen hundred weekends, and we've missed maybe ten, twenty. I stopped counting years ago.

It only works because of cooperation—mom and dad, still on the same page when it comes to being parents. When one of us has a conflict, the other covers. That rhythm—shared, steady—has never wavered.

And yes, Tyler knows when the weekend arrives. We're told he sits on the couch on Fridays, looking out the window. Waiting. Watching.

That's all the motivation I'll ever need.

If Tyler could speak, my gut tells me he knows the exact number of weekends we have missed.

And so, I walk a little more carefully and schedule my physicals with intention. I take stock of each day not as a guarantee, but as a gift.

When serious thoughts get in the way, Tyler has a way of settling me—with humor.

It's through humor that he always finds a way to bring me back—with a twist I never see coming.

Lessons Without Words

I've learned that Tyler's silence doesn't mean he's not paying attention—it means I need to listen differently.

Once, I told him it was time to leave for the mall. No response.

I tried again, tempting him with lunch—words that generally get him moving—but still, nothing.

Only when I approached—Tyler sitting at the table seemingly uninterested—did he make his objection clear.

Reaching down, he grabbed his shoes from the floor—not yet on his feet. This was his way of saying "Put my shoes on and *then* I will go to the mall with you."

I couldn't help but chuckle.

Then again, we once left the house and arrived at a grocery store. As we exited the car, I noticed Tyler's feet—just socks. I'd forgotten the shoes entirely.

Looks like he remembers that socks-only experience.

Tyler's unwavering preferences—like his exclusive love for *Toy Story* puzzles—remind me of the value of surrender.

Each Christmas, the wrapping paper hides the same gift: a bottle and cap. Tyler is delighted. I've stopped trying to outguess him.

But surrender doesn't mean I've stopped trying altogether. Every Christmas, we make a trip to Boston for a musical. It's become our tradition: lunch, a show with music and snacks, the ride home. The same pattern each year, a new show each time. Tyler doesn't resist because the structure is familiar and he loves music—even when the content changes.

I've learned that new experiences work when wrapped in predictable rituals.

These routines—quirky as they may seem—remind me that Tyler's world is built on constancy. More often than not, my role as his father is to honor that constancy, not to change it.

And yet, constancy doesn't mean perfection. I've made choices that missed the mark. But every now and then, I get it right.

Tyler's love for balloons, as you've seen, is unwavering.

I always send him back to his group home with one in hand. It lessens the burden of separation—for both of us.

More than once, as we wrapped up our time together, I'd lift the rear hatch of my SUV—and off went the balloon, floating high into the sky.

I'd watch as his eyes followed it, his face torn between laughter and loss.

But I had a plan.

I now keep backup balloons in the car.

That second balloon, inflated with a straw, always makes it into his hand.

One small solution. One decision made right.

Watching Tyler clutch that backup balloon, I realize this is what he's taught me over thirty-seven years: pay attention to what matters to him, adapt when things don't work, and find joy in the small changes that make his world work better.

He has made me a better person—not through grand gestures, but through moments like these. A balloon in hand, a quiet understanding, and the knowledge that love shows up in backup plans.

It turns out he's been teaching me all along—without saying a word.

And in learning from him, I've also learned this: love doesn't fix everything—and it isn't meant to.

Loving What Will Never Be Fixed

I didn't set out to learn this, but I have: love deepens most when it stops trying to fix.

That shift didn't happen overnight. It came slowly—through routines, setbacks, and the understanding that Tyler's world doesn't need to be changed. It needs to be understood. *Embracing Tyler's World* hasn't been about teaching him my way of life. It's been about learning his.

And over time, I've learned that once you stop trying to fix, it's easier to delight in a cabinet full of bottles and caps—ones I know will make Tyler's day.

Of course, there have been dark times—moments when I've wanted to pull over, turn off the engine, and sit in silence.

And then—just when I least expect it—"Sweet Child O' Mine" plays. Tyler's way of saying: stay with me.

This isn't a story of perfection. It's a story of laughing, crying—and sometimes both in the same breath. Like watching a balloon float out of the SUV before his shoes are even on, and still knowing the weekend isn't ruined.

Tyler wouldn't have it any other way. And honestly, neither would I.

This morning, Tyler handed me the remote control—same as always. I turn on the music. "Sweet Child O' Mine" fills the room, and he settles into his breakfast routine—bottle cap twisting, that familiar smile.

Thirty-seven years in, and I'm still learning his language. Still discovering that love lives in the quiet rituals—backup balloons, breakfast music, and the way he hands me the remote without a word.

He approached me this morning, leaned in close, and stared long and deep into my eyes. All I saw was love.

Tyler's world feels steady—his needs met, his place in our family secure. That's not a small victory.

The questions remain—about his future, and what happens when we're gone. But right now, in our home, with this music playing, Tyler is exactly where he belongs.

The remote control sits beside his breakfast. Tomorrow morning, he'll hand it to me again. And I'll turn on the music. Because some promises are made not in grand gestures, but in small, daily acts of devotion.

That's Tyler's world, and I can't imagine mine without it.

A Note from Tyler's Dad

This book began as one father's story. It exists thanks to the caregivers, organizations, and communities that made Tyler's life—and ours—possible.

Everything I've learned from Tyler—and from those who've cared for him—has shown me how essential caregivers are. They show up early and stay late. They learn each person's unique language of care. They celebrate small breakthroughs and hold hands when parents can't.

If this book has moved you, I hope you'll consider honoring this work—through a donation, offering respite care, or simply recognizing a caregiver in your community.

For our family, The May Institute in Randolph, MA, and Community Connections in South Yarmouth, MA, have been instrumental in Tyler's life and happiness.

Whichever organization or caregiver has touched your family—or is sharing this book with you—I hope you'll consider supporting their vital work.

Thank You for Your Support

About the Author

Paul Harrison grew up on Cape Cod, left the area for college in 1971, and returned in 2020.

Paul spent most of his career in the financial services software industry and is now retired. He is the father of three children, including his son Tyler.

If you would like more information or are interested in utilizing this book for fundraising, please contact: embracingcaregivers@gmail.com.

Paul does not receive any proceeds from fundraising use of this book.

Made in the USA
Coppell, TX
26 June 2026

83181196R00046